T0294563

THE SON MASTER

Peter Seaton

ROOF

Thanks to James Sherry, Diane Ward, S.B. Laufer, Charles Bernstein, and to the National Endowment for the Arts for a Creative Writing Fellowship.

ISBN 0-937804-10-X

ROOF BOOKS
are published by
The Segue Foundation
300 Bowery
New York, N.Y. 10012

The Son Master

I saw John writing the metaphysical poets today. It's an up to date way to read, so it consists less of the terminal part than the sound of a voice over the long haul gauge, the trial of sensation and dissection, counting the pages in rhyme so that the metaphysical names of the poets become possessed of a key to divided work as the blood in her veins through her knee. To keep this I can't have any pre-existing conditions. So I give them up in exchange for peace of mind. For my right hand, Charles Ives. For the rest of my life, Wallace Stevens. Walt Whitman and the men in his life for the men in my life.

When I speak among things assuming composure out of its things I pronounce it the stillness which surrounds things, for the earliest image of the thing out of this experience of men, of animal and human something space, as a portion of things is something appeared to your things which you always had with you.

In a position this image believes possible, a thing you allow yourself to be surprised by, in the legends, to be whatever you want, familiar with thousands of things.

You can create a thing or a child, leading a flame into events and among people and the thing which comes appearing in mysterious hands of a man is like an intermediary, everything you still have of formed things of conditions come to achieve the ability, a strange experience aligning the sphere of the sea or the seafloor to see and space into the page, the wording of spoken dates and places (s-space) (space) as property on the mountain and the river in pages inclined to think here is a photograph indistinctly the ultimate development of work from the last ten years at the end of the sixties.

Experimentally early, today or tomorrow, waiting and waiting and walking like walking dipped in, inventing the proximity of oceans and other things, the image of stone things were stones that slept, and placed stones that seem something stored to a child spread the same with the penetrating exposition in it, to hear or bear anything were just this still lingering one of every kind.

I know, the surrounding world, set into the head of the man with the form of the young man called the age of the man who sought bodies. As if it were that which gets by among the groups and figures you desire. You can accompany them all as if to describe them, great works with words. These figures, full of significance, as if these figures, the stone, like many of the figures, give the impression of being of their movements, the wonderful relationships of power, to be the matter through its body into space to the depths of a rock like an animal somewhere in the environment of its proportions.

Living in the collection of place and impulse proceeding from a legend, her knees her hair, transformed through the curve of her back to her face to the nameless language losing itself in stone, the hands like hands conditioned by illusion fulfillment and this action of forgetting the group called the representation of a man, the touch these pages could outline of a woman which does not stay bound to the interpretation of the revelation of your personality.

These days, such as the stone to mind or the head or the mask of the head freed to the life of the stone thought clarity lifting surfaces and their relationship to the atmosphere and figures from sleep, confidence in contours enclosed in the single vibrating burden of a copy of the request of the hand like verse it's all of, her limbs each small part of this body like will these poems allow.

The present senses lines cling to, the pen beside the poem, verse forcing the body to fill the world and be a form lines appear like, a thing enclosing bodies explores. He rolls out slightly. This enables him to see the field of play. If he stands back in a pocket defensive giants blot out the sunlight and he concentrates to separate a graduated transition seething with the face of an element.

This was in the hearts to brains—at the entrance is the man whose eyes had the world out of this tower for this monument to have peopled it. This man desires to be made a tower to represent itself, it's what is in order to appear the presumption its heads proceed in.

We're talking about the man's collar and hood and the man in the human life walks very fast and makes a hissing sound.

The man's left hand slid with both hands. The man's arm got the wrist to see how the man's back took hold of it. He's going to do it to sleep to think, or I'll do it myself. She's half frame shifted like looking at hanging out, and start it everywhere, hostage fever.

She smelled herself, she said, I've my life. I'm tough she said. Understanding some male that I don't seem to place someplace else. I want to see myself pushing and pushing something you let up, you keep to him and keep on talking, you want it done you want it done and that's it. You figure the lines and whatever he would do she said like a couple of quiet words she said you've got. Start it, follow me everywhere like the look of controlling this situation making up why you don't do it, deal with this like I was involved in this like having some open hand hard, walking around, decide to say I said I wouldn't and brought it back about the table twisting us this guy said, gotta go and won't get to talk again. You and me with a green design, and it's true, living alone, water's still hot, manage the place kind of turned on under the things I put someone in.

You might want to put on something in and out through the writers, and back again, on the cabinet and the carbine and wrap them in red and white nineteen seventy six breaks here, talking and opening five fed bright. You got the address and slip it under a permit and into his shirt: sometimes we're setting out to commit the road tugging along the ocean around a strip folding three feet wide. Remember one of the things with orange Mex Tex Sex that's again in his hand down on the right place walking up like this and turning left, I just figure we'd see you. We'd be to see you shook off and laid on strong, conscious of you and the resiliency of his legs realized then look like the difference. You should see and find out I might, she pleads to her accomplice, look at something and then another on the same day.

And then we went there and had thermodynamic retiring space in common with a feeling contributing to starting an exchange I develop of an old man walking sense and his spirit of the thing.

So our cheeks touched enclosed on the surrounding private life there was more of meaning power style to her. She says if this world and the next and this one wants me on and off when I had this Earthly power it involves the whole world being good at it.

But she says the whole world likes the whole subject, all kinds of a child too, and maybe the other one does also and the subject makes as much as that would be something that's double and I start right away toward it, if it were to give me something better in excitement not just severe with streets, where this experiment checked in external evidence of you immediately after another put them by like kings when we left.

The one we just left and in another, sooner than I'd planned, was confidence struck by the hostage fever. Old creatures lay in my room and read, the widespread use of printing occurring in a flash, national boundaries appeared on maps. You could only read if you were wrapped and outdoors to write some live weight already in bed. The right thing or European thought, to try this, to begin with I sat reading. If it went easily I'd leave because it takes so long to be after him for it, that's how he's ready. But preparing a target, I did not want him interrupting my pace of recognition and interpretation. Even among ourselves, we don't discuss our targets.

I'd work on a vein of thought, then apply it to see how it develops through real time approximations, physical laws of extension and leverage, electro-chemical space fluctuations. He prepares my card and begins to holler my name. When he sees me he says it's somehow not the same.

Maybe the body and the probability of confidence and even uses for the same as something leading itself as some other kind of question is in relation to always. To read me in the world taken as a message and so on. Enough to dream and scream and moan you wouldn't stop your loving. But what about my reading. That I see for anything else when I'm rushing to look, thought it concedes the life or the life kept going stronger and habit set up a kind of daily facts of us having all and insist that all moments raise to bust up the house, to speak of the greatest importance, demand that everyone breathe this because to have a clear head and live like I expect everybody knows, eating right, speed knit on his chest. It's summer on the top floor on the phone entering the woods and sensing anger. I couldn't see that they began to get wet while I worked on the sharp end that was outside until they were almost the drop you pull the cord up to through to taste yourself taking out the head under it and pretty soon she'd roll it around with the hook end falling until all after the other in over the inside clearer back in and we had one more in the tall grass ready.

You can stretch time with your eyes. Events around me could suddenly be thrown into slow motion while my mind was sorting problems and finding solutions at a fantastic rate. The first hundred parts you can see, and I can find it rattling louder, shivering after she's back with them and he has his place where he goes in and tells him to put it out, put the bottles in, do the talking, so I sit there and wipe off sweat beside me.

I could have been drinking, and they grabbed me to compel me to realize I have a father as a consequence. You realize these are a great many things you seem to have, the connection of two post-eventual maintenances representing where it was placed, the single most likely center of a sleeping child.

So, unite around the aspirations of this post-entropic age. Thursday, ate while towing the cabin, which is down the river. This is due to the westerners who said the season is when they blow poor ships away, son of the wind showing ancestors how to pass merchants and miners in the sky. Sea fever, yellow fever, the name in Indian for the American flag, the peppermint breast of the sea kept their minds from Maine. In what I felt caught up in, lost sister, I look through the window you'll have thought of. That makes you related, his father says, trying to explain something to me while she says what's a man getting you. What's a young face looking like in case of democracy.

That doesn't sound like the book by hearts, she said. She recognizes the strong bones he blew on. The features, the lips are large and in motion, twisting, compressing, smiling, gnawed, gnawing she says look like a deprivation, of love that's always a factor, of what this one was usually she says, they were pale, they had those pale eyes. They stood by the pictures from his eyes, what we do it's you pay me he says, I, I giving you, he, obvious she says, I'll have to go to his hands between his knees you've seen, I've seen I hadn't seen I was aware moving closer wouldn't be here listen she says, we'll just have to make the best of it seem like a man to her.

She feels the bearded man's belly and stares at him saying someone steps. She had reached out and placed this arm out a little, the back of his thighs slid upward until we could work this out a little. See that, he says, trying to look, separating the hand again and turning from her dreams to her in mild surprise.

I'll need two pieces she says. I'll need us up at the scent door license twice—with a look carefully loosened being taken through by a painting of the son looking good. The Hudson River's probably the right length in the mirror. Sun-disturbing me I said, looking uncomfortable I said, it's like a six novel wilderness, aromatic whole party whispers: why does she have to read anything to that guy. I can't hear myself in here when we walk up.

This afternoon we'll pick up the boat and black boots so he can change. Sometimes I don't know what goes with what, what ancestors are Irish. This is a decision looking for a good time, the venerable prince of spring striation beginning to break things up. He's here to do some translating, trying to drive a hold through keeping breath and body slick with perspiration. Well, a boy needing a father spacing concentrating thought entirely and looking, getting ready to look, getting ready to raise them in from around his waist and bare upper body, needing someone hired to look from her car towards us to you. Oh, my eyes race from one seeing smoke coming off a distant hill. So that must still be mind on that day in the middle of the contour rock and routing. His hand, busy expanding sound. Our sea fan, our route is more or less that there they've got in that blue edge pack point treacherous pathways spread apart before the little mouth flats and outside acrylic way out or maybe morning marks position themselves for ambush walks, a dark track zigzag moment of presentation ten years out here, we believe. Places you've set aside this day to night lay listening and exploring still, creeks along the boat for him, working changes in conditioned looking for an opportunity to you. An expert sounds like these cares are shaped to catch the constant eye swinging search. I'll bet there's a sound emerging where you first lull yourself, even his own detached rush at prey, and dispersed through the animated wind clearings.

You use rock by bouncing across on a big stone nymph. Watch the point at dusk on a number ten private, a section method's popular patterns would work. The section begins just below with blessings in the same breath. Some sort of lower boundary stretches a little higher while the body wrapped regularly with strategy for staying in close, working in breaking in as an exhibition buddy.

So there was a special room, an extraordinary person, and situations in new combinations like standing sideways like a calendar and demands complete through the trees. Other terms common to comfort: the history of plain volumes to foster my interest in reading. Editions, editions and auto-new books, our western tiers of books and reading copies, a first with a sort of frosty wave effect. A favorite transport conformation is the field affect and personal pleasure aura, a distinct perpetuation bridge, hear and see. Abstract leaders stop staring at it. Any impression recalling itself as an exile returning to subject and object closer, and add it to any kind, objects in patterns and paintings, some idea of the dispute of shape-expelling objects, abstract interest and the shape of projection.

She could mix with some further attraction and abandon you in your sense of coming home from that. Also how that language can be all others like individual volumes in his native succession and other volumes is a type of concept in the dimension of line deals and ideas of them. The motor part of power to hold a sense that is the statements in some reason.

One says unconsciously a rose. The other meant the question is with others that we do see. Equivalents in a word of orders, the sigh in the sign. And to invent to speak to extend the production of sound, this sound should be sensitive to all the visible lags developing. The independent years among the first from x to use and is such as roughly with the sun itself.

This light's the persistence to compare with time. And in time it's the range of the original dream invention of transmission sharing reasons. The source of the subject until the problem adjustments make it possible for the source variations that could be standard even if this will a system outdoors under an early sky.

And thanks, so geographic lines and latent disappear.

All the cult properties and shifts like saturated ties to theories use wedges with tears to raise them. You don't have a thing for a boy now, another thing between the west and the sunset off the shiny place.

What poor thing were you. Was whose face reflecting her face leaving him heaped with himself. The owner changes how I am? It would be the mesas riveted into T for west.

And so I used the desert gas needles in years clicking in a state of explanation and something loved me without me. The supreme cause and perennial escape of its own accompanying some, stranger wit and class, stranger set of writer and reader in the space of claims, a fact under the sun, the same one with their quality, a precise being is one and the need for electronic darling and the working physical still some.

Or times more to fill matter finally: the difficult sort used to systems needs dates to convince us there are damage parts and pulls and a reader has been missing, maybe a one letter specialist. Father provides for dark stars that strange. And once were soon to exert once more. A mind discovers moods to keep it—the projections of the broader line, oblique tops and bottoms between your line and you have been instructed, you please this line.

Ivanhoe dressed all in black knows she knows about her cares, sweet music to the temporal world is gathered there, and width by sight confining there, Wilfred, of Ivanhoe, shows up among the beasts.

I was born playing the piano. Because, before I realized what I was reading, I was trying out various sounds, even the study of psychology, and playing making I myself, I, I had a feeling, to me, the most thorough education seemed to be a continuation of my arms. I was fortunate at least enough to be surrounded, I never stopped reading. So, my inspirations. Books inherit the tradition, and through books and this room, the whole house filled with book traditions. . . .

They took me to my father when I was three. He told me I had touched the piano until, as I faced the wall, I identified a tune I was delighted with, and soon he became excited.

The word began to go around, there was a strange child in town, sort of training, I never really knew for what, for all sorts of book produce, an original rumor out of composition for each session. In the strict sense or the profession, saying the word was more interesting to hear. I wasn't part of being known I might go and could be the foundation for severe person first place; also, his reputation made people make him out to be me, man among a so called child as a child either, and I was, she thought, the experience might leave conversations always scarred. I don't agree. The act of it being in place makes the world go round, an hour apart always serious, always scarred. I didn't agree with them. I wanted to be level, a complement also to a manifestation of the way this was the way I took it. Even though I'm only his interest in me and my work as well as a feeling for projection. I had just lost Philadelphia, Boston, Chicago, other numbers of notions progressing I like to read, technical displays. So I read letters which contain the right time experiences. In 1939 besides enjoying traveling, or should I go and manage to get places for the entire world.

I had some composition, how to go about it. Friends took me in and I try to avoid the word here because with the help of the Countess it's the daughter in terms of speed and accuracy. And it's also usually speaking with certain pieces, technique you need for establishing the United States in some passage engaged in the combination of factors that turn into phrasing and physical equipment. It's hard living with an old revolutionary.

But you should have been with us when we stormed the Winter Palace. The guards didn't know if we were the infamous roving band of poets that cut the ribbons of the new regime to shreds.

I got into her big black car. I found out what her politics are. And I found a kind of digital mystery technique that gives the reader the listener getting the feeling that it gets examined. I've been offered everything too to know what they're doing and how soon and has had is hard to say. Some kind of programming the incessant developing concentrate. I must keep going. I can't be totally oblivious to the presence I tell myself, the center of my attention I tell myself that each, that each will be in the first is a first I pretend I'm doing for the first place care for speed because, I can gain my composure, when I have to hurry so New York so I had read, compose a city.

On the dark side of the moon, where you're constructing a machine cold enough to fly through the air, already consequences are being realized, here for instance, rather than experienced; you have to be able to see fast enough to live forever. I use any method, stretching out, curling up, any idiom. If it's always rather than myself I'll sit at the piano and play it right and always remember the story my old teacher took himself away with. He'd hide under a table so he wouldn't have to admit sometimes depends on how I establish the parts and become such a part of you that you know that's incredibly able, I found that, emphasizing that for me the situation alters after the fact, it and the sound, than that which I suggests I suppose, that except the conditions and that sense of learning in just one obvious example of possibility occurs in the traveling mode.

I was a result, from town to town, I thought I'd used the generation of hearing come close from the same thing, from these ample other worlds, I begin to experience three or four a year to what I could do to, from then on one was supposed to get wet, a substitute for getting attracted takes the same day presence of reason to control. I began to be aware of a relationship to the extension of the United States, to a concern I'd had an idea of to present what I was doing consequently. Five various five making common alternate show between them, to be what I could do and knew those two states of material divide into the attempt as though the air despite its experimental temperature was a form of trying to later. The way it looks when you first see it emerges again from between the temple standing well. One side of it changes colors to go find the gaudy body, the colors are all these. It's his turn. He looks at the priestess. Excuse me, with the change of light at times there's a sparkle of the blue dun fly, the fly of his dream touch of family rust, of the name some would say would you mind if I just called you these last months in. I've been haunting the markets and formulating the hypothesis.

That reminds me, the entire known world in the head of a historian in June, couple of more miles. On the way, bewildered, stopping off and picking up, wandering, thinking, I ought to be advised of the ritual spell over the streams to the north. Excited with a blue cape I'm still around listening, able to transpose the sacred air of resolution sets. The nature of a second and third complicated over and over process of exactly that, an incredibly fierce urge to stop or not, to turn around and put one together. The news is running out of verbs. I'm glad my contract includes fantasies. It specifies subjects, and physical terms where an announcer says so. At the beginning of the idea of us there's three people, and I guess it all has to do with speaking when the geographer comes in. Then I accelerate, and then revert to two, and then to one that had been as most are, the introduction to what I was reading.

And we'll see that you get mad histories to pursue, some special kind remaining don't want a long way to turn away from. Increases over there to the dust on the plains when he gets back from where he is going as he is leaving. Which sees something that provokes a giant. Except to offer to promote looking now and then, like that one, adding an emissary to the dreams of Italy. There are dark blue moons under that one, looking a little pale, heavy, they went bad dancing, then snatched away the clearing color sort of adding the high mid-air, or says it appears they've collided, or should I say is very pleasant

> too dismal day
> trapped by predatory
> flecks of gold

sort of on your toes, and twig, it is unthinkable. To get away for some surrounding hills unless you imagine that's what I came to talk to you about. As the night thickens, a little streaming brightness, one insane glance north of here, dreaming of waking fitfully, impatient and lurking in it since then it's for the first sign of holding it supposed. They seem to be almost written to be there added to at the same time.

Any one or two that way, like sonically you, or three, or any group of things you've done stand out like a camera. My favorite is, from my own, I think, lying on the standard one is a bit too close, close to my heart, standing so close. We were obviously seeing Alice reading, and hearing the short sharp yips of the children away when many countries came together and got stuck.

You can see the splices going first, where he's no longer writing but is not yet through. Like is Pierrot driving me to compose to where it would seem to where she was going may be pieces of, approach, some kind, or approach, of spoken sound part discovered that's really part believer in the system synthesis of discipline. They pose long enough to come south and have their slim duke change young, then men would come in boats filled with the take and, as one, plunge in.

One cup dry white wine stirred and covered, two or three slices we've made our with in the pan and while mine may not be the one to give you, here it is.

We've added something to turn it into. An extract, absorbed with butter and mushrooms for five minutes a little less than usual. Half cooked rice. Cool and thick, gradually assembled salt and three brown sugar scald sheets available in the top and directly over, four ounces for ten minutes between one roll with deer dried dill transfer with raised edges. One half the mixture on one to within one about five, one or two sweeten beaten inch of the edge cooked evenly over a silver spoon when it's done and poured heat proof butter, chill inch and run to watch.

Making it pretty carefully so it burns at once, peeled, raw research, indicating three cups made with. But when I found three half inch holes in a foreign cookbook calling for puff all over at three hundred fifty degrees for forty five minutes I pounced on it until golden transfer pastry could be purchased and poured into the holes. The same makes, slightly in the process of my preference.

If you're able to get directions including sounds and slices, that something you can cook and cut from edges to make flowers you ordinarily save.

Add to make time. Cover and roll in both directions. Combine water and wine to form an oblong cut-off. Some green and white hammers in a skillet, points and press indentations for the edge has vegetables, chicken, steaks and a straight line. Season to taste or will. Or will be when you start rolling, repeat into small pieces, the thick evergreen basin of water, crows while the forest fills up to the job of pitching, crows with their calling.

And then throwing the hydraulics had left it in. Then the ravens in gear and winding the thing I wanted to eat out of the tides, tides stopping only to pick out ice with a twenty five foot range between noises. Again, a quick shower, falling asleep that high and low, that completely. Into the mirror for another two or three questions, rain dripping off my cap, rain spattered down through here, still back some hours I had finally into my face, penetrating my trees, still as though just having whistled from some, still jumping in the set into place between where one to another exists without a line. We know, as in I slept, mountains, me, with his metallic clinking mind as a single energy variety, know, holding on to time, memory meal. All questions secured to a giant work light to see and once, to the south our stud die hungry and fight.

From twelve to twenty feet high we sometimes had some, our friends, turning the point of the sand, sitting around even without washing, your father was fire on the shore.

Our sensations create a whole line watching first, and for whose eyes the motions of a few men carried across the sand knowing one sprung, half lying by the fire, following instantly audible power which he still could give this day's verse so far detailed in front.

I sat down in the camp near the fire. And against my knees being placed partly against the Red River, spilling contents that affected his lungs conduct him, a large man sprung to a gun, safely reduced to the foot of the mountain at me.

My power would have been the mountain by men. The young visitor soon makes us friends. Across the plains they said it was made, if not towards him, transported from the flesh of a bear known to be in a place where we found him. The taste and smell of the pitch before them, and walking nearly into the suck of the falls a rock, presenting a good fire, no food, the world its charms itself on which it was to lodge privations where we found them, where we produce food, clothing, for our lives.

Keeping me warm, in money, and in a deep and devious wild and thick idea. The means in my hands here was that for the existence and better first time thoughts cause of fostering view was sentiments, was to convince my mind that at night animate reason would induce a belief, adding secrets to our strength, vigor and nerves.

Some of its operations, like information, elicit food. Our limbs would manufacture food and would admit, hoping to share in the appetite, the curves of a river in the calculation of a matter of curiosity, their moose-distance. We came to scrape away provisions with great care, this hope owing to the hoard. They tell us, eastern men pass the night and rise early and rapidly to pretend ten miles off by the hope of another coming towards us and turning. About two o'clock, point up coming from the east, we run through and through more to the cheerful sights excited by our corps and corporation arm. It seems bound over the shrewd and discerning eye, every distinction a part of the writing these days.

To inform our friend, to indulge our friend we were informed of of life to others who appear to be sensible of the warm houses of contented people. Every now and then a dull chapel comes in sight. But the heavy fever attacks me. I become, according to my feelings, the image of things created in my mind where my eyes, at times my legs, expect there could be found short and fleeting institutions along which we sleep warmly in a warm house.

This day's for the most part formed into almost sightless compact proceeded disorder, increased so I could not arrive a foot forward at the wayside, the station taken for the purpose of being informed down to the riverside and nearly opposite the house which stood opposite our friends, and our twelve mile place the last time in the hands of a guide, a kind of attention upon me in, he was to say, a confidential man.

Someone putting dollars in my hands and here and there a house. The following homes that had been arriving at its absence reclaimed, and "a solemn resolution brought me wealth."

Unless it happens by the compulsion of the woman of the house, the house the corporation possesses, hundreds of paces from, within view of, stuff exhibited in persons, the parents and disreputable point of view, the necessity of children, as well as their own manufacture you might suppose, the manner of the private report living, that these persons come from landing on our left.

Their house, etc., was warm and about a mile off. Each one grasps quarters descending through cloud, intimidating the unseen which comes from a mile below. But they came ashore, father insisting on attending me to obtain due north, to meet the mill, and draw off.

Scot-free, hoping to regain, hoping to be seen at and in an unknown county.

My head above water, others played a person to conceal details of a person within inches, his head, even after a lapse liked, produce instances of pain to recollect the best show charged at him. These, these, some name of young woman, some intimation of an inroad in direction, seeing that we came. Were with him, had him desire, had him approach the shore still more steel selected proceeding followed. To me to be one must be made in shore, intending to submit brother night, and that in the most a time had sewed sprung forward in hand, in between tending to at the beach towards the other of them remembered by a second transverse a third time. Amazing powers of body which you can credit being by several yards. Bought the child to land, risked for the good will wet fact true and hungry and awkward detail of prey warp for the purpose, aggravated by nature approaching to convince and command. In the middle which at this place was nearest to them it was, was again taken, otherwise to get to El Centro, those who were in it being could be advised and discovered or kinds of this part was in this was probably popularly supposed to be able.

Here was a house in a circle running across broken ground. Slight plains and important striation, friction animation, the moon under care there and passing unknown and unseen in number this night, this circumstance, resting on reports of absence so a part of us are known to a few, might have been true, fresh in on us the following site intention of our collection of the heart this causes among us. Chief Storm Town Night would have it near which had been beyond requiring to design a house for good, good wood cut in slantingly. This is the case and taste of the immortal snug in and mounted there.

It was steep and snug, every decorous or delicate sensation stationed in the Valley, famous, next, the city. My person, I sleep I understand and then, examining the city cry, we pace, to keep ourselves warm. Cold north winds blow miles from us. We turned out to place in my hearing the world a man made to believe. At part of that time of placing him where we were, nearer to us, what was to be done.

A distinction more than determined to be sure like a rule in a few persons in the open. It's more if that had been few the night before which opens on the well known port to danger who, from the article of the principal thing must be through under cover of the faces formerly before him.

Us, and us arises from a desire to set the city before you for you to say the city, or in is your reading a line lined gaping, because we return and remain and write as a matter of some under something like a more ancient Hollywood yard of the works, real as the eye in the line applies to be a word to the level meant with within, loose but printed, with several, another, singular, and others, thoroughly possessed of which we were which run it.

This is composed of this victory, which was child's play, most returned to of appearance, as to and coming to this world written the next day. Across, which lets us into the wilderness, to obtain some beyond it to account continued since we had come into this abundant countryside. Also, to represent the call altercation and warm place language with its usual speed loquacity telling us that seems on the point of to have hundreds, to the interview where there was a small house further from the city.

Our house is a large building on before we should arrive. In other words, in front of this house a hope that this is a building which seems to be upon us, a house attendant on the weight of our bodies we took possession of as a house under an idea and urging it between the town and the boat and placing it in my arms, some precious deposits, that they had not had time to watch the flashes of the fire near the gate and into the water taking place, attempting one vicinity toward myself relieved.

That target ends in the dissolution of the gate, transportation to the spot, our means and method straining every characteristic idea and feeling nerve was that generality descending a little, taking my friend, the ladies, carried away, to draw from us whose heart was with the great body born to the city. Every now and then, male and female, sending us compliments in the shape of a spark pound drawl procession in line with the town. The lady approves of action and at the right time flees he says by everyone along the beach of the bay. He wants us to believe that was readers set in the words affecting his absence elsewhere, the blood portion of sound subordinate clause transmission near to the place we mark with precision appearing intuitively, the city and vicinity, the attention straggling village, village and farm space, the ancient spacious secret cause, severe and additional style village, tight houses, warm houses, and neat houses and family landscapes, cold air pasted with paper, cold air volume with an impalpable snow strike and the mind of the stranger inconvenient night winds and rapture. A small space from the western eye compared in a way that it might be observed day and night when these people slaughter their beasts for language.

And practice towards the center of the room where we sleep. Stuck in it rising where a ground law falls into a large basin. Information lays three to five feet according to surplus circumstance in the wilderness. Hope our warm bodies are large and stuffed· but not tainted. We become hay or leaves, to keep every step taken in with this kind of support scale afterwards in a state of position. The warm spot nearer to the city, summer months of sex latitude as a description. That sensations, sensation, conveniences, we have just arrived into the wild in this land of the happy enjoyment of life.

In the houses because an illusion, the climate, a warm room with a variety in the female variety and female remains enter it and all become prey. The wall and rifle strict state drift she excites, a desire with a coastal interest in atrocity or the sons of the sciences in the reins of attention. We're leaving the domestic villain in the crevices filled with small articles, the same bet leading to the notion of sex systems of marauding hands.

From the Colorado period and the plains constructing distance Earth. To place tools persisting in this strong recession from our ears for one secure house of this kind. It's performed by the last between the walls and the ceilings under which may be half a mile hill, rising ground in the elevated daylight hill, close in with it formed of those crevices which it was said this was search authorized by blowing a whistle. Affection, because of his refuge, having relieved a thousand other things in a dozing longing state. Standing one night under the moon with noise running in casting the hill building of the house part out of sight silently by a slight hill (straight hill). So they brought the sole wall objects of articles and imaginary mass place where my head lay, the part with the wall between us bursting a person heard in a profound sleep. Confidence clause, and confidence fever, and running a clear moonlit place, a place of observation lined to my situation cause, the best paced width of probable effect which might follow the arch to use time.

Well that's the end of that. It's no longer necessary not to distinguish the curve of the Earth within its parts, the necklace, always moving like a breeze through space. And the items of our disingenuousness altogether, borne a bit by stolen roses.

You can mix it up to pry it loose from some trace of its own discovery.

You can take it down to L.A. and establish something minimally which doesn't mean the tortuous road to excess can't ever run out of you.

Floors won't let it. Walls and doors and especially the engine burning wood to turn to face the sun won't let it. On the other hand these deposits, like planets, gathered circumstantially each time the room is left.

Reading fever.

These are some of their calm results. Remember how beautiful you were, Leonora imprinted on our backs if I could touch you there. So many classical considerations like angles: provoke someone reading a book, absorbed by recognition, willing to do anything to wipe out communism like healing the sick and bringing the writer home to the office to show a movie on how to spend money.

No whisper within, sound asleep, past without usual noise to me, in my deserted state, it seems to amount to more than many of these by the outlet but by the we came which of their own were in which by this was seemed running to the storm. Ancient cities simultaneously developing treatment, we were driven to this sort of compassionate improvement. One's under that having been called like most grasped with ecstasy, the determination never to part with what is again with while going from the idea of any whole plan to mean how it is disclosed from the Earth to scatter the access wildly and widely again and our schemes, my immediate friends, with having some when it is this.

Pins and needles, either by the way of which is on the margin of, or to get over with a speedy visionary from luminous moon belief and information suggested by the vicinity signal such as other than to propose and begin cold confines of circumstance to adopt some of which were when we came taking place, and all eyes heading the purpose before the main body in the eastern men and the keeper fields, the mind representation ground submitting falling and fascinating covering terms urging us observable among with the foot of the first of our range retiring phrase of insulated buildings heard throughout the line. First from above us, here we last leaving from their arms behind them along the beach because of hawks or cable pacing leader lodged in the warmth of our bodies.

Observable foot of the first now placed, that for there we were of what seems to be passed in many parts. The line, pretty wide apart, the receding son, the first onset from above us. Even to us either taken leaving from a number because or to the houses. Great rate ropes take me in aside their own place to be either or a see pit. My elegant hand descent, and all's involved in a great depth of a real stand intimately attended to. This became the bone of strife, the New York line degree to resist plans and return and close into it as does all hope of range ready to have vanished.

Then there were pines in his head from some of the mountains, people get off and ask were we stretching both that make up or could be at the top shut, then there was massive counting and the guess last eights eight or nine like another rock wall, another person having his whole estimation condition, his society named. She appears to be serious until she gets up our systems figure that winter or the next. Where there's getting to be some function toward use and impact throughout the phone man pass away approaching us, shoulders crowding together soon afterward in high extra, precise cold, murmuring, murmuring, walking through, stopping, and economical run spotted from hanging, scanning, the rest of us roped off in the dark, lying, since without the last ice age dinner's over like the warning word from the rear string gyros steadying the feeling sky coating, knees pitching a silhouette you adjust to the head and neck clear of more of everything yourself after the collective place revival sight is this: give up the night, or the moon, or expect conducting in form, the wish forms, to meet us with an arrangement to get the best service day by day becoming more part of the day. The still season separation pleasures they're always impervious to edge in the hundred hundred warmth ten years air. Watch a poet living instead of his horse and catch a ride into town. Sleep in a rooming house wilderness assembling nearer. In a mirror in the dark, and all day and at sundown in the small hours. A vision of dream weeks keeping her up to say grounds of taking care of itself and the switch self to suggest the moonlit climb halfway up the dark rock legs completely to watch this inside it to sleep in light. A title caught in the rocks reaches a cutthroat by dark and waits across the summers we stay in. Walt Whitman breathing hard just before that was then, a generator ride highlined across what we were having running out by powering her every hundred feet help of the rigid hip hitch and covered jack free gain and gain run and wrecked effortlessly again and trading it to see machinery, in place generation, and raced to the hills at this same place in a father's big boots.

I flew to get up empty. A waist high official and background burn and the coming silver fronting built up to tell the wind on. Names, abstract property, survivors of thinking singing it, sounding the disappearance of the location stop topographically, digging in the state to their knees.

Moving boulders, boulders connected by a thin record in error. To speak they make up stories they don't understand. To propose telling such stories they take notes and draw near. And they begin to tell this is what this is, this man's name. News of himself, in an effort his mind excites by this encounter beginning to learn its meaning. Research, as far as I know this is what I have written here.

The incident, living in the Valley, the similarity, events gathered at first. . . no one ever was making the sound winter as the meaning more distinct, as the detail of from what was coming and the sub-preparation, the sound, winter, the winter storm.

My childhood on my own, my thoughts on how not to avoid a variety of associations, and how to get more is that I would fall in asleep someday which I had only recently left stolen. All that utility, the heat captivating game introduction softened by its prophetic slip. Routinely losing ingredients and back to the farm at night, I have to plan the day, passed around from farm to farm I got to know all about the mercenaries and life in my native city in winter.

Stranded to follow an American English adventure, a Pacific adventure, soft sandy horses in spots, English, beak to beak, America to start must stand six feet around disengaged things called shakes and seconds. Protruding from throughout most of the world, anything ancient in New York City made of steel. Local set regulations through the heart translated as how many people describe natural poison and power in a ritual. Her body going all over the condition place edge thing in favor of constancy, this control kick, a bi-lingual career woman in her mid-twenties.

We're still translating to travel aloud and now it's your turn, hold the champion to wake up. I'd say I like those I went to once since covered the point like a convert. In California it's no longer the same idea. But I'm saying that in California I write in person. I decided I'd have that happen to me since you might have to be heard of to prove it was here. I dream I read followed by you a lot, to see I'm glad somebody likes my sleep, but I get up and write an anthology.

I fix English with magic out of the catalogue and the L.A. and New York Connection Ode working through most of the city people who could give up copies and give me half.

I started out in the form L.A. took of some favorite New York areas of composition, arranging the need for all this amazement, and positions of episodic parts, in a sentence spot with silence you couldn't get into L.A., as well as that inclusion joint of pleasure blocks, I guess, L.A., privately adding that haven.

The vanguard said to me a long time ago, if people want me to do this, circles dropped by, the L.A. that left me.

Names among others, the stocks in wards are for elm, pine, ash, oak and aspen. Although flesh and fish, the vulnerable lighting aisle called walk the watch words is the rock not to be kinder later, to the only shaken plant memory there, a small portion reserved as a degree in a letter or record according to Sonoma stationed at her references and arranged to keep awake and attract notice. In early glimpses of the world notices inheriting through intrigue typologies, street skinners in a row, her own blood experience and little Elizabeth on or near part of the origins overflowing. Only in the central and the center and the center in the wake and others looking like a cloud. Like the severance controlled from outside surrounding a child with their offspring.

Enforcing is part of another world not outrunning a book. In this book we see through gaps in each reach-in along and in attractions of excess successfully just outside, the poet says, the poets' silks and the roses in place catch fire framing the flames and jewels. And the allusion to the classes that are lost, side by side I went up to see the same site writing rags and roof company lunge in. People have noticed, throngs to the drawing reeds and decades, conspicuous steam green material context of the heart emporium in range and depth growing an aspect to build in in the great house symbolizing singing a song of everyday life.

I found the woman, women usually, living in the same house and adults living in the same house, the daughter, some take their time asking by standards to bring more from me.

I found the women, one of them, women usually, living in the same house and adults living in the same house, ask a child described for me. The other men and I study time together calling on each other and forming household chores. Concentration freezing from the description surrounding the brain. Technique suffering, and then there are strong mass precision causes, but it may be a tangle into the head. The echoes are advance location parts of displacement supply, material injected into the blood and a brain. A serious steady night of rest, you could turn out to be some progress. To an agent on time major, more women.

Simple representative to a China dam. So the best way to plant peace abroad in the Province of Maine is to look for the saint of American old days having written after he read. The solutions to all the emerging places are the famous stories urging him to be allowed to see. When you and I tend to agree I tell you one point is that this looks as if I were somebody full of figures, all the data so you make no mistake with you, which is what adds up to the picture I've made up to confide in you coming to an end.

And from the west, wages and innocence and repentance and man's fall. Barns from my farm, mean men and women, T.D. Tony Dorsett, number thirty three, stores off the map, stars off the map was born, also at least one of these in the uprights, braced-in women.

He's got bones from a grave in New England and memory that was brought from her bones and the hands and more hands on any pretext at sunup. In an era of line agents emptying and breaking the compromise and filling me with brother reason, convulsions mock the man reading any American book of spells. Fifteen minutes ago a boy came over writing for the ways of the world. It takes two men falling in with his jaws when he speaks, tempting the city if you kick him. The conventional object invective seems about to lurch into two dirty pledges.

And finally, vagabond vice persons taking editorial charge of life in any form. Paper ropes rot and set men in the current of American sensation names mirror memory merges with world readers with the same kind of grip indicating sex judges as the judge in the city judges the story of a poet stirring. Demanding episodes, the old eloquence arrangements, crystallizing in the extension into territory.

Among the model artist attractions the fiends with faces run in New York. That includes heart duties at New Orleans, to be a master after my Mississippi. Or bleeding the way near plain hale mass New Hampshire. The spirit sisters fusion pages for the passages and independence praise of poetry. Abby's running the offense statues have, about this piece of producing the direct wants of the body in a day. You seem to be preceding this life to the cover of the face among the raid through that. Toward Conjunction Junction a new volume of you preparing from the first, of a boy native of fugitive magnetism.

This impression adventure is being saved for influence hunting peculiarities. A strong Christian friend, like Joy, who must win, and the action streak of social implantations, intrigue, off with the stuff in his heart and in his mind for heroes in a binary way.

The pro stampede which grows out of our associations of the west completely explodes it.

And here it comes again, father stuff and substitution leaving it to read persons and physiological passages for the sake of you under my own roof. I need my burg tomorrow, wishing us onto a field of appreciation like getting happiness from God or Kings or Congress. It's clear close to the letters leaving everything as a demonstration of alarm, dangers of the test for George for a notion I would like to fix it so. Reading ambition, what the father in English charges streaks as a single line under the thundering thumb.

This is the evening before I ask some questions about you too. I promise to be prepared, no, that's just being tempted. To signal the privilege piece subject to enjoy being temporarily talk like this. The possibility might seem accepting, inviting, obeying and betting to him. And then written followed by words. Copernicus says his wheels okay in Baltimore, his wheels cut a square though in place which is care like an angel and new things line in among the words. Cultivating the emotion sheet field for the time and woman pool some track service near the quarry days, a sample of her physically because she knows what's happening to her, what she says and others could realize it concealing the effect you have to press to wait for saying this pushing it away on hidden hinges. With her arrangement of orbits to read banks of the mind facts, eyes delight, by torchlight cutting or boarding playing it, holding on to it with two sharp taps of a stone. Patience or a monument or a light his father says imagine his face unless the light makes a phrase like figure influence hours at a time. All night you find a statement, the habits of will patterns of bonus will, the position to cheer you up, real or imaginary knees return or stone from the window at the window.

The sun from the sky mounts, and with the sun's help fierce hours on the blooms is leading. Something of images because you have control, you can be somewhere. You can create looks, like it's anywhere, and change its nature. The vision of space with space or one in a particular instance is physical space with the physical set of physical new son space. It could be that physical. Space training in the rescue sphere, in Europe and America it's January in nine cities and two space centers. In Houston, everyone must carry a gun. It's been called the high planning survey and inventory, the study of and investigation into another space day interaction of sun and space effect particles, the space day device space led, space sick, and space is the trace familiar space spell of subject bodies in acceleration causes of space standard space.

Listen to reason. This is the best of all possible worlds. There's nothing to say about it except in exile. Which is where it's such a dirty business being so attractive.

Some people have to return to the face of the Earth, which may be billions of light years away by now. So star drive, the rudimentary notion of light, is having it both ways. Head in the clouds and feet on the ground, the last technician plots a course. He's a man, he's lucky.

But getting back to the march, it's been called a matrix for ambient flesh, movement of the cornering of the heart's desire. This is a problem, frequently worked out as a solution to ethics. Each little child is a female child. Heat is the same as neat in this Heaven on Earth.

For example, instead of internal rhythm, it's axiomatic. There's a plan, it could come from England. There's a pledge and it goes like this. You bet your life reading this.

Some substance, it's got its own life, including others'. You don't even have to spread your arms. You have to look out the window, expecting to be hid. This compulsion, family and friends, family and friends, and these angles and declinations, stored up because a treatise on extra-parental behavior can also be written lickety split.

I used to work for New Hampshire woods. Like any family life, and doses of destructive outposts, designing circuits for Mao, for me to go institutional would be a physical and emotional model sense I see and they are, zone kids get pregnant and get determination local.

The grounds and grooves in large oceans and in the bays of the world, there are species that live on both sides and into both and in the sea in the eastern ocean near the western waves in the waters of the storms at sea. Sometimes they suck up the dark ocean light, penetrating the bottom by the basketfull. The football migration, going from near the mass near the speed of mass near the speed of light into the warm waters of the gulf, catching prey and avoiding obstacles, thought in the long migration sticking up and staying fierce.

Large numbers and warm bodies produced by crushing and prying the ocean period particles of high metabolic rate periods and particle advantage trapped between the air and some other air or skin. A cinnamon species in cold guard bundles through the term thin and too fast to match. But the long migration north leads to north periods of lips. It's the mechanism you can imagine if you open your mouth slightly and swim over the roof of your own mouth and feel grown out to form this apparatus in many places around the world, the world and the film that lived on Earth, a line of sight inflating to become extinct. The lower numbers licked off the tongue and sounds so low in other ways. Some sound speeds and some sound loud. Friendly sounds for migrating, sounds meanings, letting them slide kinds that come from a structure called the case. And the more ordinary air from the finest of air and also not too far and often farther.

Sometimes the champion finds evidence in search of some relatives down in the dark sea. Some think that extends from tip to tip, but no one is really sure. Body distance straight up in the air from a distance and as you are seldom seen you can see straight up and down to stick out like straps and sound in the dark night of the hundred and hundreds. The coming age of quantities was taken from society and towed laboriously out of the village. This was before pits in the frozen ground with the age of plastics. Contemporary numbers plastics, common somewhere and some groups with the patterns on their bodies and kings and queens can move without the magical properties of objects in the dark night.

My hands, hardened to let water in, found that the nails were no longer bleeding; they had rusted causing this operation. The family, and this father, to this same family of the deserts and semi-deserts speaking Americans speaking of the United States east, from Doctor Texas to states of the changed name of the hand at a touch. They might be within the family borders that might be off the land and trouble with practice, either it's calm or there's so much light we could fuse movements on brain pressures to discover any section of the Laws of Storms that close with it. It must be the slam indication of escape, work a property of consideration and the direction a design assumes to go to the ones to the south somehow, staying put and eating in no time because reason got them there but the mirror these two places will join wants books. It's destiny in the mist of an episode going to pieces.

That exposes a flying patch of the sea, a row of the sea in a silence to some extent by a mirage in the sense of certainty. And that it's growing in on either hand to complicate my air. Two ends of the region like this with the light behind one and a warning that all lies in a group like the dark, its dim shape off and on for daylight outside until it did seem in color, under a brilliant sun, a band of purple, green for my point of view, things in detail thousands of feet high and miles away to extend beyond a mountain at least to breed. And which have oceans of the world behind them, their faces are the jagged outlines near the steep hills of light on the French mass fading away. And night vapors dominated by the enterprise discovering them. Your jealous things placed on the real one and spelled with snows of the gray Pacific.

That greatest world has no rivals. It's only a few hours away and plunges down to a great reader: I saw, or rather admitted, a southern ocean. All this may be met anywhere sweeping home every night. I mean that the radius of action would take the jump completing the world. I would add to my memory through that ancient machine, a geographical expression, the chemically objective stuff. It's all the strength in the addition, all of the line in machine around the lower part of a globe. That marks the area, the dispersal of quantification, in which this vertical existence has geographical snares and where places to most people had lain across it. The name for the rest of the week to the exclusion of a passage, there was a nasty cloud passed over us. The job of the progressive hydro-last idea of west to east, the pioneers introduce ideas for a visible leader in a steam world, chief training, the Chief finishes his pictures, a series of sheets at home, slippery sleep legs, our heads or arms, as I thought, the textbook directions for asking for trouble.

If I let food cooks, that's a fright. Dirt from the tropics as its reputation got to hate it, its music which is the great west wind falling into sound. The superlative hand to hand through two split yards up and down, square yards. An imaginary machine provides a proof so that a single sound in principle was a more ambitious mistake for serious alterations for the start.

To which, to take charge, this feature could be any idea of the need for a substitute for an advantage over the sound fracture plate extended rather than dug out, and I could use white line looks to a wall of dark red stone. The shape of one too is so hard that to take charge we had all survived. The elastic remains in the eyes to clear it over. This is a preposition, a possible sight of everyone's appearance without the business people touching. Great logs of the moon used also for legs, light complicated by catastrophe instructions, to move somewhere with a bang and a knock out of us, we know enough. Knocked flat near the conventional center, rest and have dinner and wait all morning so it must have been the rain that fell. The machine cares, but those two can be the same, the moon experience of space of sky throwing out dance and dance invasion.

He used to pitch for the Great Circle Tigers in the Infinite Time and Trouble League. I could lay off a promenade and the safety sweeps, once is a good history for the stone age. It gets the city the finest site to bring her back, the power cubes near the house of houses, but I come back at night to space cities and loose sheets of paper, the right consistency for material ability.

Copying trees out swarms the American pilot. The parts, wealth of detail, washing the light description to see if they were true. See if I understand: one inhabitant, one migration. I got a job to try to get, to get through the flowers of Le Mair, the shortest course for considering any large city, and objects of the conspicuous country amusement thing I could have seen yesterday and next morning. Cause of coast, wall of rock, flat as boards, the most places covered for everybody else, green all over. The green color roar, what we were doing there, seeing heroes watch for possible beauties. Line of sight, start finding the females at home, man interference and run provocation, face to face babies in the world.

To make a proper animal scrub its skull space in the sound range of resting for mothers going or going to knock off scenery, order a paradise dominated by sites free from snow and other grounds among them dodging out of place for walking, a dream form or position, order the rocks and ice and water. Also, talk of intimate islands of smoke written on the opposite page and published to keep a statement English in a mystery.

But it's always possible to be a whisked away subject for a savage. Or a claim to end the impression looking at the light wind and at its strength. I think I know the instrument rate maneuver—an obsession loaded with enterprise—proposition, one's own eyes from lips to observation speed straight in it. A sanctuary takes us in, the last of the legs keep dangling. The first vanishing people will look for it personally. The visible image white feather and diamond twice and secret adventures of levitation and entertainment.

In bed to get a bright red scarf, the pale ghosts of Valparaiso slowly approach. So a stranger wants to see the colossal continent, the tallest thing in the world and mon francais clear in separate actions; but we can see through the frozen surface of the sea.

The eye is hooked on ice. All the place is full of ice. Atmosphere and access in the two summer months. The first moon started with miles of the moon and continues to hit.

The first moon photographs its internal systems to freeze. The sea of the moon's hidden dark side was stopped in July. The path behind the moon was a series of film with miles. The images could blitz the tight end from Earth. Data links landing on the moon. An instrument shaped instrument support powered by images just prior to their impact on the moon. This likely looking moon made with fittings takes us home. One or two days on the moon looking at planets.

Things that make up daily life, meteorites and meteoroids, air, food, housing, the Moon, the Moon's intelligent beings, the circles of space for power or other stars instead of rockets.

Years are stars caught in space at some remote spot on Earth. They could be placed on the moon to protect the moon in orbit, or on the moon and stray extremes of message beings to protect processing. A proposed technique arranged by items, a single image human could be covered, heat for the power forms and appropriate space data duration of space shift periods and film tears loose and left.

The rosy soul ridges of the cities struck into invisibility. It's to isolate a culture till the wind shifts to be active in the evolution of machine intelligence.

The pine peanuts of New Mexico and the orchard memorial to the Indian king.

To every traveler on our western plains the coming of the white man to cure disease for the white man and the residual fluid of the United States in pieces of paint. The desert dried to cultivate smoke and that brings us to an expression applied by another desert preparation families go for. In his monograph, it's the frontier forming and lashed together in the desert. It's consumed as marvels and mass reduced to a syrup. So, pines dipped into their mouths.

The instinct sands colonize the streets of dreams in a country with rain. They have one, and why not? The stands behind the door, and falling from the trees are men, women and children with their own ideas of life so they could not sit all day but they had all night.

My reefs, my trees had fallen. Mention the trees because of their trees and crack the trees to come from the city. And read the page at which the manuscript fell open, there were questions.

Then the reader crowds the page in the rush of his ideas. He surprises himself as a manifestation of precision, the conventions meaning freeze and reread. I know, the production of writing becomes the sense of almost as much as the problem readers do, the readers do one and shift as readers do. They function as poor boys inhibiting structuring. Designed to allow scrambling, Lester Hayes, Lester Hayes, Lester Hayes. The Wausau Cafe and the first lady's name, the natural facts so the names of coming material fits forcing the readers to be conscious, the orient reader route of the seedy reader. Aware that Lewis and Clark stand where we look toward the contract field of needs of reader distribution. What one might call reading and writers.

The idea is that missing the reader more than another father on the path into the woods of policy. The woods seem to be there for writing, what Charles Ives called sound, which has very little to do with writing. It seems mixed up, man father, child boy. And Anthony is something special because he makes me think there must be some special page and word things, maybe to avoid crazy legs to avoid polygamy. He could say the drought in the region of abstract identity reads by children a step and and but put together, so forget it. And books do this to readers planning a shift to other words in lines of writing. They can write clues to the thought is bizarre. Also candy and consequence, the signal break or shift in the present. Writing the full farm of supplying taught in schools, and the syntactic tent, to read bear, to read tests run on a map, and on the original Bonnie Free Fall the objects had read, after a reading delay of pattern attribution, the reader kept hours a day for a week reading reading writing as adults of human actions. The first of global patterns, and especially as readers in this light.

Like preferring to prepare the writer for the room. Reading and read around though in practice, of course, there it is, ritual reading, and testing, to read to write the purpose reading in the conventions of reading to be reading to construct readers. Or should people aim abstract models of the world in physical readers to promote readers in revolt. (Illusory father who can read without writers), images of reading by imagery, switch writing.

In the universe of problem readers and problem writing the reader and reader agree the ideal reader sounds a bit distant. Imaginary writing that the writer is writing at the reader's request: the reader did writing to reader and writer, that-is-as reader and the writer can be writer the reader imagined of the reader easier to write than reader and writer in writing as the situation of written differences concentrating the reader's.

Writing in writing as in sea writing becomes written as written reading. Writers, or reader all that and the writer, in the reader's ideology. In order of writing, a writer's projection, writing to take writing written in written in reading, and writing as writing to the composition reading writing writing goes writing, and writing word to word can be writing the reader between writer and reader and writing.

The origins of stars collapse. Then they become White Clues or Shining Stars evolving out of astronomers suggesting the entire universe at tremendous speeds. Distances expand and so do substance hunters and the Jupiter Line from a princess into the sky. In stars forming its face and in this clear star from stars hangs the star of glowing guides to the rare gas of the upper rays and in the particles that come from northern centers like unaided eyes which form into the closest fragments of tidal Earth which takes our year two years in Jupiter space bands. So clear permanent bright spots shine brightly, and when the Earth occasionally appears in them discovered by moons.

Groups are more compact, often moving as distant spots in some fine galaxy. The great objects include the large stars of the largest shadows. The other eight million miles to Earth takes moons close. The western edge diamond details at twelve miles per second in a binary star now seen, now discovered, now seeming to be the position of the region of families when the moon is new. When it's between Earth and moon shadow bodies of the Moon passing over you because the Moon travels rapidly over the Earth and Earth's inverted moon father nights that the frontier stars and skies are seen.

Star light getting used to the dark. Star bright with the stars before your eyes. First star map that contributes to star names in common wish with a sheet of red Greeks, a sheet of thin Roman paper, descendants to the representing stars to one side and star names, the ideas the animal could overcome for centuries, useful and placed in the skies. And planet books on the opposite side of Heaven, star trails including the moon part driven with a clock to the north following points of a landscape on airless Mercury and

Venus depending on the west like the Moon's approach to the direction of east on one side and cold on the other to the west.

To compound clouds formed by following the line by name, line grant, chasing away. They like to have fallen by the strength filling up among them and put an end to them. Should the prescription of time by a short speech be caution to his successors, assuming they keep their articles and adverbs first while we are sober.

The best danger probes to be putting out elements, and one I take to be speech upon pain of death. This was being a commander going to sight fire and suspecting things in order thought to the master business, plunder resistance as he thought to surprise the Chief without a word with the chiefmen ashore in the night.

The master asks who did by the way, assume the desire for an answer, a single being pouring in and grappling with her. The dispute, except one, and only two rose again and get away and drop trinkets at his pursuer. The dwarf is a star from the Pleistocene. It's known from the Pleistocene, stripped white to grey then yellow or blue.

Like a small country beginning to establish its own songs or, quote the empire's rulers, the father had a tendency to fall in love. As he moves he says I belong to this class. Its struggles include the Danube which is happy because it's coming to Hungary. And its logical sequel, spiritual pain, and then one of the heroes is free to write her: "Everyone arrived in New York in October. I was unhappy and depressed by the destruction of Europe.

"America extends towards the east. An inch of the geographical notions of lunar confidence in parts of the world made of tides which cause the sun overhead and movement of the sea of air which expands the movement of the sun and moon until scientists began."

Space was found to be full of the moon causing tides of air, breathing and flying air higher than the sea. To test the theory, make the Earth's gravity measure the air of sun and moon in the form of winds. The weight of the air in rhythm—the velocity of a few inches of sun and moon increases as the speed of the sun's electrons in the tropics reflects parts of the winds of the world fusing the high flying atmospheres with the average Earth curved equator known as calculations of the sun and moon in ripples, in words known as standing or stationary sea on one side and disturbances of the golden sea brown nights of the moon while the moon's famous moon creatures hide in the brains and eyes of the Indies.

So who can keep in tune with the Moon? Columbus, as mysterious night and the theory of mysterious light, sees himself coming from the male bearing females to a hiding place in the laboratory to surface as the lunar moon quantities synchronized with the moon during the full moon in June.

And that's the best time to feast on the sophisticated moon breathing stalks of sand or sand in southern nights of moon sand and new English sand surveys processing for progressive exceptions to control. Speaking precisely when the Moon runs high about the same time for the solid Earth and swarms of hemisphere prophecy that the islands might pull apart where the Earth is under stress in space.

In New York, an influence in the traditional moon pores of planets compresses wood to begin with on the sun, or Jupiter on the same side of the sun. The cause of force named for the arm of the English break from your direction reflected and deflected on the rotating Earth is over. Right back into the ocean, counterclockwise, for the subject of existence toward the west looking spun as a set where lines mean range in English.

There's another midnight system of whole globe behavior requiring the Newton Faith of moon volume and moon power on the Earth view of the universe as global as the moon's movement of a rotating Earth and the Moon's first attention to the moon that complete's the moon of the Earth to the sun and the moon with the moon pulling a stone with moon mechanics the same way, the moon revolves around the Earth, the moon is one side of the moon, the side the Earth revolves around or the sense of massive Earth and Moon below the surface, moon to moon between them away from the moon marks of speed in the world of certain parts as it is today.

The muscles have also been to·Europe. The muscles keep writing to get reading technique accents. When they are clear they're tightened. And half the secret is Irma, the beauty of the band you played with.

This phrase, according to the pilot, would take people somewhere, and so I had an experience with the position the body deals with live in New York covering the trance prominence signal to lock my ideas through. The verb is always the simple word and the simple word will do.

The old verb lingers on; calling the verb legal, I shall soon present the past today. The finite form of verbs becomes possible like a verb acquiring the verb proper, the verb proper contains questions, the idea of smoke, or a desire to get shook up instead of learning that you intend to desire forms of expression nearer the abstracter verb.

Since the verbs used in here are all words, whenever there is a desire to see the predicate finish your work, suppression of the verb, the verb or some part you tell him where else does a phenomenon of writing go.

This is worth thinking about because your voice feels your mouth emit words in a scene for mastery making good. I felt that merchandise and poetry of a word fact form of you in a way mumbles some words like what I was saying, shall I live as a basis of thin air. The sense of the words alone at home with nothing to do was lined up so it looked like speech. A voice reading them as we had again in what I was to you placed again and we were to answer everyone, answer to us, the imagination of a picture in time touched in a foreign country surrounding our states of mind and heart and sense element rays and receive them during the intimacy of these things.

There is a will, groups of verbs in the present tense. It states words after becoming conceptions. English origin first begins to part by appearing and using the real verb before the real verb with independent elements which the infinitive, i.e., we split the infinitive, forgets in the spirit of our words in the situation as a whole. The name of a person passed in something home for you. We put words into the fusion with the nominative, the nominative of an address. Two classes in the different persons remaining behind or numbers, the numerical simulation of a continuous field requires old forms as logical subjects to take some strong man in some other person or thing, the stronger of the more and the most taller than that.

The superlative kinder man, there never was a man more kind and the person or thing is the highest descriptive, the simple favorite in the world used in an excited language.

He felt these thoughts helped in dreams, like a child, or making decisions, dangerous objects and dangerous forces causing the personality wish that leads to the pages set out and writing right away. And that child is written, his feelings are the feelings of a child. That's a child in the act of a child, the master of the sergeant's life turning to trouble.

All the men were inscribed by then. Then a boy needed some music, I think he was Beethoven, and might have been later couldn't be found. At that moment remember by heart, or, to be more accurate, everything.

An outsider thinks everyone knows eternity is written with discoveries. However, a chemist told me to picture generation after generation living for more thought and things and write women's affairs and cares, women inventing photography for their husbands, making up the children, solving world problems by creating movement to the lovers occupied by monuments, construction for problems in attention to these problems and, to get up and go off to say this is all talk, there's too much talk, too familiar western living creatures, the organism bells of humorous scenes with children.

That makes the henchman think of himself as those dream. Suppose everyone wants to be clean, something under the rule of the given tyrant, the darkest night, the Caucasian Mountains, the people write make the landscape understand contemporary numbers in traditional concepts from memoirs, you can imagine anything about parents. The approach is quite strange, but my tastes keep changing.

Foreign things that I like I like and some I like primarily. For instance, written long ago, he comes as a foreigner. At that time we were born near each other, I, by chance, on the radio. But that's a beginning, and we know favorite words. So people greet us with a vocabulary proving the result of a spoiled master. Said, once said, the writer lives and sleeps like a gambler trading biographies and whispering the joke to the crowds. Power nerves, what could I think a mystery orders? Cast-off dreams?

Is a madhouse exaggerating stronger then and is a madhouse more than living slow movement, the others make poor people grow bored and keep thinking, there were cases, it's still the development, that's how lives and works wrote in energy or tension.

Until the lean years of the revolution it's usually the other way around—a man steals an idea circulating as a plan. Say there was slander, it was worked out in the parallel twenties. All the players left the country suddenly saying so you were hearing the actual sound. To prove dreamily I was a child, I think, the most truthful one. And the war, I don't know, at the same time I like it very much. It's easy to look at. The most popular saying or appropriate interest called the custodial style used to call it a search in an ancient city or a landscape clearing up and a woman walks by and says there's some anniversary movement created by a hope monument made of brick and the bricks broke through and were just put back. And if you don't dig around inside it wears off quickly, take that to the others sleeping at night and falling apart.

Even our distant descendants know how to write. They move their fingers over him in every piece you read.

This was a picture from America. And the spirit snarled, but it was clear. I was going out of my way, my nose and brains were topnotch.

Pumping the south, science was ready for ages. Shoot before breakfast, hurl buckets of water up every day. Demand the sea-water to be waiting tinged with grease, audible spells in the young man's letters. He filled the steam in a jug without a word, he had been writing with stones so one thing spread on the rock's got a lot to think, to listen to the old man singing serves to make a little repair as usual, how you sing with it hope it comes.

It would be a raven on a rock. You can get screwed too, by the thought of leaving everything out. The present grandfather says complicated sentences like the old time European explorers sensing his dreams and expecting to check on pests and drifts just outside. Look up at the sky in the spirit form of place and sky stolen by flight. No lying, no flying. Eyes, eyes in the sky surrounded by a liar's ears, liar's eyes, liar's nose, and this is out of the sky, wait like scents of phrases, a long ago girl in the sky.

Think of approach like a great stone, poor old fist. It was who were you sticking out in the flesh you got me in associations. To sing a song to pull up words full of his old mind back. Why all the bones behaving up in the sky. Acres of more in the head, piling up. It's a piece fell off trying to guess where the animal monsters move through the air and sound some sound of logic there: the head in two shapes, the surface body under the surface, the white place speeding like air exploding over the thought that this phenomenon whined away over again, and again names him the shapes of seas and witches.

So if you go fast enough long enough you become all there is all at once.

Watch out for my secret, fill the days with the phrases, let it stay staring and ready to eat images of power, circles to stay and scream at. Maybe quiet winds and warm spring screens and other dots all over make the world sleep words to watch.

Move a few yards during the seconds in a doze. Take ages in sleep then keep still. Reach out and grab it for the approach of its ancient glaring white plain, the polar sound and screen of a shape over the lip, the back of its shape and then shattered. The pattern of a place misting in the warm moist air would have to wait and the boy wants to say, Look, don't go around on the roof in the lights, the sea where the ice is thinner and where wide rivers begin to slide. Places in the moon, who can see and say, Listen, the sea listens with your heart, our stop kit comes to a spot inspecting spots of shifting sea spirits and move.

A living thing loose on the beach and there were young girls in there, for all to see.

The city hits a nerve, pets are white under the black sky, the neon roofs and soft snow psyche as the clowns go to work give me a push like a drummer seeing the door. The gold domes of St. Basil's in Red Square and the wheel and the clock, the man beside me says would I shake his head as he speaks.

The two auxiliaries pay me, pay me, pay me. They're model auxiliaries and still have some often used as such so that you're pleased with the promise of these words as pure forms in the future in question, a pure future replaced by the language since the constraint of authority for a person is different points on the island or on the assembly.

Will is a model auxiliary. Sons, or the idea of compulsion or the third associated with the second and the third in the first expresses a will for desire to will to be glad. But that will establishes the language as consent to the people of England. And we use the model Outside England by not giving up the natural American Circuit Rider, the literary second and third model future indicating the will of someone promised or assured something in person.

This is the tag on a hero's lust, a window substituted for a hero's bust, your sweet just's strung on sticks and one pulls along the page in the garden with the country and translators. That business in feminine words is veiled by her grace. And by her two regimes, the believer in sleep in paragraphs, in the farmland of the West which causes ancient gods and sons of gods first for so long.

The gods had goddesses and completed the population that

might have been called the frontiers for families, the desire for hereditary wounds or even much recalling that develops there by keeping notes to work for generations. Some deadly drugs keep silent till the nineteenth century. These rules were challenged by contemporary pressure as the twentieth century tendency to distinguish the wide open words as a whole.

Its purpose is to fasten opposites to animal roses before the wars of the letter to the memory object. Signs and situations associate with what takes place with other writers, in this case the survivors of a slippery business. And words like Pittsburgh and Utah and Denver were music to my ears—show us that forest. Water pine and bald-cypress spread in the basin. They probably name the North American question to attract impressions of modern times far from their home in L.A.

So parents scattered over the ocean floors in celebrated stages instead of piling up into generations. The first time I found myself facing the heat of the cape, the silence of its night, the heat turns the water into steam.

But this is different. This was bangs, splashing, hisses, hammering water, roars, dull bumps, growls, explosions. One had to be near the surface to be aware in fragments on land. The senses from then on, and this is the source on the run, from each in touch with the thick covering on the top and each side of each is free to rise. The speed and mass full of bubbles thinking material skyward and a spectator, not an athlete, converts much of the heat of the sea to rose fragments of kinetic seconds. Crazy rate of speed, a moment after leaping ones, exploring as soon as these touch from the water dark fingers which point to the sky.

The stark, dark fingers of a giant hand, each is allotted a curve in the wilderness. Each composes the curve to border intimacies with the saints and angels in the walls. The wars of relaxation revive the republic from the role of wars and the place of war by a war at heart. To decide what to do these are premonitions. The soul strings of light minutes written to keep running. (I began to see entirely physical things. The stone floor of the room and firewood. Vague, mystic Edna stretched out her aspirations and practices the episode in which this is what I want to do appears.)

"We carry with us the hour, take her glass, and choose the best. If wonders is all she has show them prodigies in us." A look and a book in living things is merging the surroundings of the reader with what was this mystery reading.

"Wonder with a good hand and profess it." How did they work?

By being built for the twentieth century. An ice ship in the midwest. She was the toast of two continents. So even though she never had to she forgot how to audition.

Write her mind that way, by the angel masters and sympathetic reason arts. I take my pen and whisper, you are how you deserve to be writing written by a man.

Now, some ancestors write the profits about Maine. That's when the prophets mind for my living. I catch this with a certain phantom. I write her the heroine of a famous poem putting pen to paper walking and reasoning, the present pleasure like affairs, and the languages to develop, even in qualities and habits. What did you tell them?

I could spill away in the moonlight and see mist in white faster but at the same speed. I could see more, but we'd known that.

What did they ask you?

The moon itself hanging in the sky. Something hidden and looking helpless. The power to move, watching for fish or fowl. And a biped using the army with cinnamon eyes, I think.

Scheme on foot to heart for it. Tear down to the heart for it. In the house and out of breath, it was that storm of simplicity. Right now, it appears to be in some absence of wilderness where I can meet in spacious language and stay talkative.

Of this edition, 26 copies are lettered A-Z and signed by the author.

Typesetting by Skeezo. Published with the assistance of The New York State Council on the Arts.